TRAVEL
BUCKET LIST

This book belongs to:

_____

_____

_____

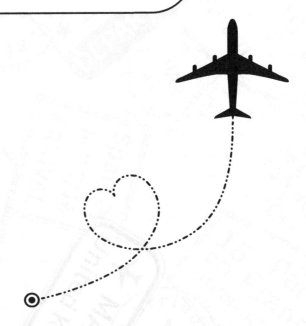

ENJOY YOUR Journey

THE BUCKET LIST

Destination or name of Your Trip

01	☐
02	☐
03	☐
04	☐
05	☐
06	☐
07	☐
08	☐
09	☐
10	☐
11	☐
12	☐
13	☐
14	☐
15	☐
16	☐
17	☐
18	☐
19	☐
20	☐
21	☐
22	☐
23	☐
24	☐
25	☐

THE BUCKET LIST

Destination or name of Your Trip

DONE

26 _____ ☐
27 _____ ☐
28 _____ ☐
29 _____ ☐
30 _____ ☐
31 _____ ☐
32 _____ ☐
33 _____ ☐
34 _____ ☐
35 _____ ☐
36 _____ ☐
37 _____ ☐
38 _____ ☐
39 _____ ☐
40 _____ ☐
41 _____ ☐
42 _____ ☐
43 _____ ☐
44 _____ ☐
45 _____ ☐
46 _____ ☐
47 _____ ☐
48 _____ ☐
49 _____ ☐
50 _____ ☐

I haven't been everywhere but it's on my list

Colour all the places you have been to.

01

(Destination or name of Your Trip)

Priority ☆☆☆☆☆ Solo/With _____

WHY

HOW

RESEARCH INFO *(websites, magazines, etc.)*

Estimated Date		Budget	

I DID IT!

Date Completed		Location	

MY STORY

How was it? ☆☆☆☆☆

HIGHLIGHTS

MY THOUGHTS

Pics / Memories

Would I do it again?   **YES** ☐   **NO** ☐

02

(Destination or name of Your Trip)

Priority ☆☆☆☆☆ Solo/With _____

WHY

HOW

RESEARCH INFO *(websites, magazines, etc.)*

Estimated Date		Budget	

I DID IT!

Date Completed		Location	

MY STORY

How was it? ☆☆☆☆☆

HIGHLIGHTS

_____
_____
_____

MY THOUGHTS

_____
_____
_____
_____

Pics / Memories

Would I do it again?   **YES** ☐   **NO** ☐

03

Priority ☆☆☆☆☆ Solo/With _____

WHY

HOW

RESEARCH INFO *(websites, magazines, etc.)*

Estimated Date		Budget	

I DID IT!

Date Completed		Location	

MY STORY

How was it? ☆☆☆☆☆

HIGHLIGHTS

MY THOUGHTS

Pics / Memories

Would I do it again? **YES** ☐ **NO** ☐

04

(Destination or name of Your Trip)

Priority ☆☆☆☆☆ Solo/With _____

WHY

HOW

RESEARCH INFO *(websites, magazines, etc.)*

Estimated Date		Budget	

I DID IT!

Date Completed		Location	

MY STORY

How was it? ☆☆☆☆☆

HIGHLIGHTS

MY THOUGHTS

Pics / Memories

Would I do it again?   **YES** ☐   **NO** ☐

05

Priority ☆☆☆☆☆ Solo/With _____

WHY

HOW

RESEARCH INFO *(websites, magazines, etc.)*

Estimated Date		Budget	

I DID IT!

Date Completed		Location	

MY STORY

How was it? ☆☆☆☆☆

HIGHLIGHTS

MY THOUGHTS

Pics / Memories

Would I do it again? **YES** ☐ **NO** ☐

06

(Destination or name of Your Trip)

Priority ☆☆☆☆☆ Solo/With _____

WHY

HOW

RESEARCH INFO *(websites, magazines, etc.)*

Estimated Date		Budget	

I DID IT!

Date Completed		Location	

MY STORY

How was it? ☆☆☆☆☆

HIGHLIGHTS

MY THOUGHTS

Pics / Memories

Would I do it again?   **YES** ☐   **NO** ☐

07

(Destination or name of Your Trip)

Priority ☆☆☆☆☆ Solo/With _____

WHY

HOW

RESEARCH INFO *(websites, magazines, etc.)*

Estimated Date		Budget	

I DID IT!

Date Completed		Location	

MY STORY

How was it? ☆☆☆☆☆

HIGHLIGHTS

MY THOUGHTS

Pics / Memories

Would I do it again? **YES** ☐ **NO** ☐

08

Priority ☆☆☆☆☆ Solo/With _____

WHY

HOW

RESEARCH INFO *(websites, magazines, etc.)*

Estimated Date		Budget	

I DID IT!

Date Completed		Location	

MY STORY

How was it? ☆☆☆☆☆

HIGHLIGHTS

MY THOUGHTS

Pics / Memories

Would I do it again? **YES** ☐ **NO** ☐

09

Priority ☆☆☆☆☆   Solo/With _____

WHY

HOW

RESEARCH INFO *(websites, magazines, etc.)*

Estimated Date		Budget	

I DID IT!

Date Completed		Location	

MY STORY

How was it? ☆☆☆☆☆

HIGHLIGHTS

MY THOUGHTS

Pics / Memories

Would I do it again? **YES** ☐ **NO** ☐

10

(Destination or name of Your Trip)

Priority ☆☆☆☆☆ Solo/With _____

WHY

HOW

RESEARCH INFO *(websites, magazines, etc.)*

Estimated Date		Budget	

I DID IT!

Date Completed		Location	

MY STORY

How was it? ☆☆☆☆☆

HIGHLIGHTS

MY THOUGHTS

Pics / Memories

Would I do it again?   **YES** ☐   **NO** ☐

11

Priority ☆☆☆☆☆   Solo/With _____

WHY

HOW

RESEARCH INFO *(websites, magazines, etc.)*

Estimated Date		Budget	

I DID IT!

Date Completed		Location	

MY STORY

How was it? ☆☆☆☆☆

HIGHLIGHTS

MY THOUGHTS

Pics / Memories

Would I do it again?   **YES** ☐   **NO** ☐

12

(Destination or name of Your Trip)

Priority ☆☆☆☆☆ Solo/With _____

WHY

HOW

RESEARCH INFO *(websites, magazines, etc.)*

Estimated Date		Budget	

I DID IT!

Date Completed		Location	

MY STORY

How was it? ☆☆☆☆☆

HIGHLIGHTS

MY THOUGHTS

Pics / Memories

Would I do it again?   **YES** ☐   **NO** ☐

13

(Destination or name of Your Trip)

Priority ☆☆☆☆☆ Solo/With _____

WHY

HOW

RESEARCH INFO *(websites, magazines, etc.)*

Estimated Date		Budget	

I DID IT!

Date Completed		Location	

MY STORY

How was it? ☆☆☆☆☆

HIGHLIGHTS

MY THOUGHTS

Pics / Memories

Would I do it again? **YES** ☐ **NO** ☐

14

(Destination or name of Your Trip)

Priority ☆☆☆☆☆   Solo/With _____

WHY

HOW

RESEARCH INFO *(websites, magazines, etc.)*

Estimated Date		Budget	

I DID IT!

Date Completed		Location	

MY STORY

How was it? ☆☆☆☆☆

HIGHLIGHTS

MY THOUGHTS

Pics / Memories

Would I do it again? **YES** ☐ **NO** ☐

15

Priority ☆☆☆☆☆   Solo/With _____

WHY

_____
_____
_____

HOW

_____
_____
_____

RESEARCH INFO *(websites, magazines, etc.)*

_____
_____
_____

Estimated Date		Budget	

I DID IT!

Date Completed		Location	

MY STORY

_____
_____
_____
_____

How was it? ☆☆☆☆☆

HIGHLIGHTS

MY THOUGHTS

Pics / Memories

Would I do it again?   **YES** ☐   **NO** ☐

16

Priority ☆☆☆☆☆ Solo/With _____

WHY

HOW

RESEARCH INFO *(websites, magazines, etc.)*

Estimated Date		Budget	

I DID IT!

Date Completed		Location	

MY STORY

How was it? ☆☆☆☆☆

HIGHLIGHTS

MY THOUGHTS

Pics / Memories

Would I do it again?   **YES** ☐   **NO** ☐

17

(Destination or name of Your Trip)

Priority ☆☆☆☆☆ Solo/With _____

WHY

_____
_____
_____

HOW

_____
_____
_____

RESEARCH INFO *(websites, magazines, etc.)*

_____
_____
_____

Estimated Date		Budget	

I DID IT!

Date Completed		Location	

MY STORY

_____
_____
_____
_____

How was it? ☆☆☆☆☆

HIGHLIGHTS

MY THOUGHTS

Pics / Memories

Would I do it again? **YES** ☐ **NO** ☐

18

Priority ☆☆☆☆☆ Solo/With _____

WHY

HOW

RESEARCH INFO *(websites, magazines, etc.)*

Estimated Date		Budget	

I DID IT!

Date Completed		Location	

MY STORY

How was it? ☆☆☆☆☆

MY THOUGHTS

Pics / Memories

Would I do it again?   **YES** ☐   **NO** ☐

19

Priority ☆☆☆☆☆   Solo/With _____

WHY

HOW

RESEARCH INFO *(websites, magazines, etc.)*

Estimated Date		Budget	

I DID IT!

Date Completed		Location	

MY STORY

How was it? ☆☆☆☆☆

HIGHLIGHTS

MY THOUGHTS

Pics / Memories

Would I do it again? **YES** ☐ **NO** ☐

20

Priority ☆☆☆☆☆   Solo/With _____

WHY

HOW

RESEARCH INFO *(websites, magazines, etc.)*

Estimated Date		Budget	

I DID IT!

Date Completed		Location	

MY STORY

How was it? ☆☆☆☆☆

HIGHLIGHTS

MY THOUGHTS

Pics / Memories

Would I do it again? **YES** ☐ **NO** ☐

21

Priority ☆☆☆☆☆ Solo/With _____

WHY

HOW

RESEARCH INFO *(websites, magazines, etc.)*

Estimated Date		Budget	

I DID IT!

Date Completed		Location	

MY STORY

How was it? ☆☆☆☆☆

HIGHLIGHTS

MY THOUGHTS

Pics / Memories

Would I do it again?   **YES** ☐   **NO** ☐

22

(Destination or name of Your Trip)

Priority ☆☆☆☆☆ Solo/With _____

WHY

HOW

RESEARCH INFO *(websites, magazines, etc.)*

Estimated Date		Budget	

I DID IT!

Date Completed		Location	

MY STORY

How was it? ☆☆☆☆☆

HIGHLIGHTS

MY THOUGHTS

Pics / Memories

Would I do it again?　　　　**YES** ☐　　　**NO** ☐

23

Priority ☆☆☆☆☆ Solo/With _____

WHY

HOW

RESEARCH INFO *(websites, magazines, etc.)*

Estimated Date		Budget	

I DID IT!

Date Completed		Location	

MY STORY

How was it? ☆☆☆☆☆

HIGHLIGHTS

MY THOUGHTS

Pics / Memories

Would I do it again?   **YES** ☐   **NO** ☐

24

Priority ☆☆☆☆☆ Solo/With _____

WHY

HOW

RESEARCH INFO *(websites, magazines, etc.)*

Estimated Date		Budget	

I DID IT!

Date Completed		Location	

MY STORY

How was it? ☆☆☆☆☆

HIGHLIGHTS

MY THOUGHTS

Pics / Memories

Would I do it again?   **YES** ☐   **NO** ☐

25

(Destination or name of Your Trip)

Priority ☆☆☆☆☆ Solo/With _____

WHY

HOW

RESEARCH INFO *(websites, magazines, etc.)*

Estimated Date		Budget	

I DID IT!

Date Completed		Location	

MY STORY

How was it? ☆☆☆☆☆

HIGHLIGHTS

MY THOUGHTS

Pics / Memories

Would I do it again? **YES** ☐ **NO** ☐

26

Priority ☆☆☆☆☆ Solo/With _____

WHY

HOW

RESEARCH INFO *(websites, magazines, etc.)*

Estimated Date		Budget	

I DID IT!

Date Completed		Location	

MY STORY

How was it? ☆☆☆☆☆

HIGHLIGHTS

MY THOUGHTS

Pics / Memories

Would I do it again?   **YES** ☐   **NO** ☐

27

Priority ☆☆☆☆☆ Solo/With _____

WHY

HOW

RESEARCH INFO *(websites, magazines, etc.)*

Estimated Date		Budget	

I DID IT!

Date Completed		Location	

MY STORY

How was it? ☆☆☆☆☆

HIGHLIGHTS

MY THOUGHTS

Pics / Memories

Would I do it again?   **YES** ☐   **NO** ☐

28

(Destination or name of Your Trip)

Priority ☆☆☆☆☆ Solo/With _____

WHY

HOW

RESEARCH INFO *(websites, magazines, etc.)*

Estimated Date		Budget	

I DID IT!

Date Completed		Location	

MY STORY

How was it? ☆☆☆☆☆

HIGHLIGHTS

MY THOUGHTS

Pics / Memories

Would I do it again?　　**YES** ☐　　**NO** ☐

29

Priority ☆☆☆☆☆ Solo/With _____

WHY

HOW

RESEARCH INFO *(websites, magazines, etc.)*

Estimated Date		Budget	

I DID IT!

Date Completed		Location	

MY STORY

How was it? ☆☆☆☆☆

HIGHLIGHTS

MY THOUGHTS

Pics / Memories

Would I do it again? **YES** ☐ **NO** ☐

30

(Destination or name of Your Trip)

Priority ☆☆☆☆☆ Solo/With _____

WHY

HOW

RESEARCH INFO *(websites, magazines, etc.)*

Estimated Date		Budget	

I DID IT!

Date Completed		Location	

MY STORY

How was it? ☆☆☆☆☆

HIGHLIGHTS

MY THOUGHTS

Pics / Memories

Would I do it again?   YES ☐   NO ☐

31

(Destination or name of Your Trip)

Priority ☆☆☆☆☆ Solo/With _____

WHY

HOW

RESEARCH INFO *(websites, magazines, etc.)*

Estimated Date		Budget	

I DID IT!

Date Completed		Location	

MY STORY

How was it? ☆☆☆☆☆

HIGHLIGHTS

MY THOUGHTS

Pics / Memories

Would I do it again?   **YES** ☐   **NO** ☐

32

(Destination or name of Your Trip)

Priority ☆☆☆☆☆   Solo/With _____

WHY

HOW

RESEARCH INFO *(websites, magazines, etc.)*

Estimated Date		Budget	

I DID IT!

Date Completed		Location	

MY STORY

How was it? ☆☆☆☆☆

HIGHLIGHTS

MY THOUGHTS

Pics / Memories

Would I do it again? **YES** ☐ **NO** ☐

33

Priority ☆☆☆☆☆   Solo/With _____

WHY

HOW

RESEARCH INFO *(websites, magazines, etc.)*

Estimated Date		Budget	

I DID IT!

Date Completed		Location	

MY STORY

How was it? ☆☆☆☆☆

HIGHLIGHTS

MY THOUGHTS

Pics / Memories

Would I do it again? **YES** ☐ **NO** ☐

34

(Destination or name of Your Trip)

Priority ☆☆☆☆☆ Solo/With _____

WHY

HOW

RESEARCH INFO *(websites, magazines, etc.)*

Estimated Date		Budget	

I DID IT!

Date Completed		Location	

MY STORY

How was it? ☆☆☆☆☆

HIGHLIGHTS

MY THOUGHTS

Pics / Memories

Would I do it again?   **YES** ☐   **NO** ☐

35

(Destination or name of Your Trip)

Priority ☆☆☆☆☆ Solo/With _____

WHY

HOW

RESEARCH INFO *(websites, magazines, etc.)*

Estimated Date		Budget	

I DID IT!

Date Completed		Location	

MY STORY

How was it? ☆☆☆☆☆

HIGHLIGHTS

MY THOUGHTS

Pics / Memories

Would I do it again? **YES** ☐ **NO** ☐

36

Priority ☆☆☆☆☆   Solo/With _____

WHY

HOW

RESEARCH INFO *(websites, magazines, etc.)*

Estimated Date		Budget	

I DID IT!

Date Completed		Location	

MY STORY

How was it? ☆☆☆☆☆

HIGHLIGHTS

_____
_____
_____
_____

MY THOUGHTS

_____
_____
_____
_____
_____

Pics / Memories

Would I do it again? **YES** ☐ **NO** ☐

37

(Destination or name of Your Trip)

Priority ☆☆☆☆☆ Solo/With _____

WHY

HOW

RESEARCH INFO *(websites, magazines, etc.)*

Estimated Date		Budget	

I DID IT!

Date Completed		Location	

MY STORY

How was it? ☆☆☆☆☆

HIGHLIGHTS

MY THOUGHTS

Pics / Memories

Would I do it again?   **YES** ☐   **NO** ☐

38

Priority ☆☆☆☆☆ Solo/With _____

WHY

_____
_____
_____

HOW

_____
_____
_____

RESEARCH INFO *(websites, magazines, etc.)*

_____
_____
_____

Estimated Date		Budget	

I DID IT!

Date Completed		Location	

MY STORY

_____
_____
_____
_____

How was it? ☆☆☆☆☆

HIGHLIGHTS

MY THOUGHTS

Pics / Memories

Would I do it again?   **YES** ☐   **NO** ☐

39

(Destination or name of Your Trip)

Priority ☆☆☆☆☆ Solo/With _____

WHY

HOW

RESEARCH INFO *(websites, magazines, etc.)*

Estimated Date		Budget	

I DID IT!

Date Completed		Location	

MY STORY

How was it? ☆☆☆☆☆

HIGHLIGHTS

_____
_____
_____
_____

MY THOUGHTS

_____
_____
_____
_____
_____

Pics / Memories

Would I do it again? **YES** ☐ **NO** ☐

40

(Destination or name of Your Trip)

Priority ☆☆☆☆☆ Solo/With _____

WHY

HOW

RESEARCH INFO *(websites, magazines, etc.)*

Estimated Date		Budget	

I DID IT!

Date Completed		Location	

MY STORY

How was it? ☆☆☆☆☆

HIGHLIGHTS

MY THOUGHTS

Pics / Memories

Would I do it again?   **YES** ☐   **NO** ☐

41

Priority ☆☆☆☆☆ Solo/With _____

WHY

HOW

RESEARCH INFO *(websites, magazines, etc.)*

Estimated Date		Budget	

I DID IT!

Date Completed		Location	

MY STORY

How was it? ☆☆☆☆☆

HIGHLIGHTS

MY THOUGHTS

Pics / Memories

Would I do it again?   **YES** ☐   **NO** ☐

42

Priority ☆☆☆☆☆ Solo/With _____

WHY

_____
_____
_____

HOW

_____
_____
_____

RESEARCH INFO *(websites, magazines, etc.)*

_____
_____
_____

Estimated Date		Budget	

I DID IT!

Date Completed		Location	

MY STORY

_____
_____
_____
_____

How was it? ☆☆☆☆☆

HIGHLIGHTS

MY THOUGHTS

Pics / Memories

Would I do it again? **YES** ☐ **NO** ☐

43

(Destination or name of Your Trip)

Priority ☆☆☆☆☆ Solo/With _____

WHY

HOW

RESEARCH INFO *(websites, magazines, etc.)*

Estimated Date		Budget	

I DID IT!

Date Completed		Location	

MY STORY

How was it? ☆☆☆☆☆

HIGHLIGHTS

MY THOUGHTS

Pics / Memories

Would I do it again? **YES** ☐ **NO** ☐

44

Priority ☆☆☆☆☆ Solo/With _____

WHY

HOW

RESEARCH INFO *(websites, magazines, etc.)*

Estimated Date		Budget	

I DID IT!

Date Completed		Location	

MY STORY

How was it? ☆☆☆☆☆

HIGHLIGHTS

_____

_____

_____

MY THOUGHTS

_____

_____

_____

_____

Pics / Memories

Would I do it again?   **YES** ☐   **NO** ☐

45

(Destination or name of Your Trip)

Priority ☆☆☆☆☆ Solo/With _____

WHY

HOW

RESEARCH INFO *(websites, magazines, etc.)*

Estimated Date		Budget	

I DID IT!

Date Completed		Location	

MY STORY

How was it? ☆☆☆☆☆

HIGHLIGHTS

_____
_____
_____
_____

MY THOUGHTS

_____
_____
_____
_____
_____

Pics / Memories

Would I do it again?　　　**YES** ☐　　　**NO** ☐

46

(Destination or name of Your Trip)

Priority ☆☆☆☆☆ Solo/With _____

WHY

HOW

RESEARCH INFO _(websites, magazines, etc.)_

Estimated Date		Budget	

I DID IT!

Date Completed		Location	

MY STORY

How was it? ☆☆☆☆☆

HIGHLIGHTS

MY THOUGHTS

Pics / Memories

Would I do it again?   **YES** ☐   **NO** ☐

47

Priority ☆☆☆☆☆   Solo/With _____

WHY

HOW

RESEARCH INFO   *(websites, magazines, etc.)*

| Estimated Date | | Budget | |

I DID IT!

| Date Completed | | Location | |

MY STORY

How was it? ☆☆☆☆☆

HIGHLIGHTS

MY THOUGHTS

Pics / Memories

Would I do it again?   **YES** ☐   **NO** ☐

48

Priority ☆☆☆☆☆ Solo/With _____

WHY

HOW

RESEARCH INFO *(websites, magazines, etc.)*

Estimated Date		Budget	

I DID IT!

Date Completed		Location	

MY STORY

How was it? ☆☆☆☆☆

HIGHLIGHTS

_____
_____
_____
_____

MY THOUGHTS

_____
_____
_____
_____
_____

Pics / Memories

Would I do it again?   **YES** ☐   **NO** ☐

49

(Destination or name of Your Trip)

Priority ☆☆☆☆☆ Solo/With _____

WHY

HOW

RESEARCH INFO *(websites, magazines, etc.)*

Estimated Date		Budget	

I DID IT!

Date Completed		Location	

MY STORY

How was it? ☆☆☆☆☆

HIGHLIGHTS

MY THOUGHTS

Pics / Memories

Would I do it again?   **YES** ☐   **NO** ☐

50

(Destination or name of Your Trip)

Priority ☆☆☆☆☆ Solo/With _____

WHY

HOW

RESEARCH INFO *(websites, magazines, etc.)*

Estimated Date		Budget	

I DID IT!

Date Completed		Location	

MY STORY

How was it? ☆☆☆☆☆

HIGHLIGHTS

MY THOUGHTS

Pics / Memories

Would I do it again? **YES** ☐ **NO** ☐

TRAVEL
BUCKET LIST IDEAS - WORLD

01	Get stunned by the Great Pyramid of Giza / Egypt	☐
02	Check out the Mona Lisa at the Louvre in Paris, France	☐
03	Walk along the Great Wall of China	☐
04	Visit the Colosseum in Rome, Italy	☐
05	Hike to Christ the Redeemer in Rio de Janeiro, Brazil	☐
06	Be intrigued by Stonehenge in Salisbury, England	☐
07	Enjoy wine under the Eiffel Tower in Paris, France	☐
08	See a Santorini Sunset from Oia in Santorini, Greece	☐
09	Visit the Acropolis of Athens, Greece	☐
10	Enjoy a performance at the Sydney Opera House in Sydney, Australia	☐
11	Climb Mount Kilimanjaro in Africa	☐
12	Admire the aurora borealis in Norway	☐
13	Search for Nessie in Loch Ness in Inverness, Scotland	☐
14	Watch whales at Saguenay-St. Lawrence Marine Park in Québec, Canada	☐
15	Ride on the Orient Express across Europe	☐
16	Safari in Kenya	☐
17	Sleep in an overwater Bungalow in Bora Bora	☐
18	See the Taj Mahal in India	☐
19	Take a Gondola ride on the Venetian canals in Venice, Italy	☐
20	Swim in all five oceans	☐
21	Fly across the Atlantic in a private jet	☐
22	Visit the Galapagos Islands	☐
23	View a fashion show in Milan, Italy	☐
24	Watch the Sumo Wrestling Championships in Japan	☐
25	Go to the ends of the Earth	☐

TRAVEL
BUCKET LIST IDEAS - USA

26. Listen to Jazz, Try Creole Food and stay at the French Quarter in New Orleans, Louisiana ☐
27. Fall in love with New York City ☐
28. Feel the Mist of Niagara Falls ☐
29. Lern to surf in Hawaii ☐
30. Go gambling in Las Vegas, Nevada ☐
31. See "the Heads" in Mount Rushmore, South Dakota ☐
32. Have Fun at Walt Disney World in Florida ☐
33. See Someone Famous in Hollywood, California ☐
34. Learn about American government in Wahington, D.C. ☐
35. Visit Yellowstone National Park ☐
36. Bike across the Golden Gate Bridge and see Alcatraz in San Francisco, California ☐
37. Have a Gospel lunch at the House of Blues in Chicago, Illinois ☐
38. Sky dive over a California desert ☐
39. Watch the Northern Lights in Alaska ☐
40. Stay at a five-star hotel and upgrade your room ☐
41. Attend the Burning Man festival in the Black Rock Desert, Nevada ☐
42. Go skiing in Aspen Highlands, Colorado ☐
43. Drive the iconic Route 66 ☐
44. Climb the Statue of Liberty in New York ☐
45. Train as an astronaut at Space Camp in Huntsville, Alabama ☐
46. Ride a motorcycle across the U.S. ☐
47. Dig up dinosaur bones at the Dinosaur National Monument in Colorado ☐
48. Go to the Super Bowl ☐
49. Celebrate Mardi Gras in New Orleans, Louisiana ☐
50. Go glamping at Joshua Tree National Park ☐

DOODLES

DOODLES

DOODLES

DOODLES

Travel

DOES THE

Heart

- GOOD -